May sweetness permeate your soul

May sweetness permeate your soul

Lilya B.F

EDITIONS AKHAWATES

AKHAWATES Editions ©

ISBN : 978-2-494885-89-9

2024 All rights reserved.

Printer: Amazon

editionsakhawates@gmail.com

To all my sisters in Allah, this book is
for you.
Your sisters dedicate these few words to
you.

This book has been reviewed by two students of science, wishing to remain anonymous, who follow the Quran and the Sunna of the prophet ﷺ according to the understanding of the pious predecessors.

They affirm that there is no error of belief (Aqida) or any ambiguity in this book. Therefore, it is not discouraged from reading.

I disclaim any misunderstanding on the part of the reader.

May the Lord reward them with good.

Salam aleykum wa rahmatullahi wa barakatuh
May peace, mercy and blessings of Allah be upon you.

Often, we are in need of advice. Yet, nobody takes the time to offer it to us.
This book aims to provide you with what we would have loved to receive...
May this reading be as sweet as your hearts.

May Allah preserve you and love you.

Perhaps we write because that is the only
means we have to express ourselves and
recount our sorrows.
Anonymously, perhaps because we are
ashamed of who we are or what we have
experienced...

Our stories are our escape, even though we are
part of a large community.
Mutual aid is beautiful, but it is even more so
for His sake.

Let us put down our pens and papers and, for
a moment, look at each other, listen to each
other, and offer advice because, indeed,
His words are full of advice for those who
listen carefully.

Fraternally, S.

Do not let others' darkness cloud your heart.
Always aim to be kind and compassionate to
others. The good you do will surely come back
to you, brightening your life. May your soul be
filled with gentleness, turning you into a woman
with a big heart.

Do not lose hope in His mercy. Your
exceptional behavior will be rewarded
accordingly, in shaa Allah.

*May the Lord of all creation guide you a to be a
righteous woman.*
آمين

Preserve yourself, sister.
Embrace modesty, chastity, and discretion.
This way, your value will significantly
increase. Do not expose yourself to the eyes
of all.
You have no need for the opinions of others
to measure your worth. What matters is
His judgment, for He constantly watches
over you.

Your deeds and what lies within your heart are
never hidden from Him.
Strive to honor Him, submit yourself to Him.
Respect His commands, for all that has been
ordained for us is solely for our good.

**Have you ever seen a precious jewel
exposed to the eyes of everyone
without protection?**

You are a precious gem that must always be
preserved and protected.

May Allah the Most High place you under His protection.
آمين

Constantly remembering "qadar Allah" in every
situation is essential in the life of every believer.
Fear should not taint the continuity of your
existence.
As long as you have the Lord of the Universe
in your life, you have nothing to fear.
Place your complete trust in Him, for His
decisions are always right.
This worldly life will be simpler and more
serene, and your destiny will be easier to
accept.

Do not let the devil distract you from this
wonderful relationship you have with your Lord.
You are much stronger than you think!

P.S: Do not forget to always recite your
morning and evening supplication to
protect yourself from any harm in shaa
Allah.
Of course, these are only means...

Stop holding onto people in your life who no longer want to be part of it.
Love is not enough, and that goes for all relationships... especially friendships.
You should walk your path only in the company of those who offer you respect, esteem, consideration, attention and so forth.

Surround yourself with souls genuinely concerned about your well-being, souls that care for you, souls that simply contribute to your happiness and fulfilment.

Know your worth and do not let anyone convince you otherwise.
Take care of this soul that belongs to our Lord, for it is to Him that you will return.

May Allah make you a woman endowed with wisdom and a vast heart...
آمين

Do not let grief, as painful as it may be, distance
you from your Lord.
Use this trial to draw closer to Him and cling
to Him.
In the end, He is the only One who will
always be there. So, place your hopes only in
Him.
He will never let you down.
Shaytan loves the sadness of the believer.
So be brave and fight it.
Sorrow will fade with time and patience,
do not worry.
Everything in this worldly life is ephemeral.

Today you weep, tomorrow you will smile,
Do not fear what will come, because He is with
you.

*May Allah soothe your heart and bring gentleness and
peace within it.*
آمين

Never tire of forgiving,
For you do it for yourself above all.
It will allow you to finally be at peace with
yourself and with others.
It will keep you away from all the negativity
that conflicts bring about.
Forgive, even if your heart has been broken.
Do not let grief or a wound chain you to
resentment and desire for vengeance.
Forget all that.
Rely on Allah and forgive.
This does not mean forgetting or repeating
certain mistakes.

It is good for you, believe me.

*Who are we not to forgive when the Most High
never stops forgiving and being Merciful
towards us?*

*May Allah enable you to forgive all those who have
wronged you, so that peace may reign in your heart.*
آمين

Do not expose your sadness to the whole world,
because this same sadness must be preserved
to avoid being exploited.
Do not give malicious individuals a
weapon against you.
You have the best listener by your side,
as Allah hears you.
He is with you and always will be.
Listen to His words, as sweet as honey,
to soothe your heart.
Confide in Him, for He is the One who heals
sorrows.

Patience, troubled soul!
Everything eventually fades and gets better
with time, even the biggest wounds.
Remember, within difficulty lies ease.
Put your trust in Him, He will never let you down.

*May Allah grant you the patience you need to
overcome your trials.*
آمين

*"For a very long time, I had the feeling
that sadness would never leave me.
and that happiness did not want me.*

If you find yourself in the same situation,
you should know that the closer you get to
your Lord, the more you will see the
positive side of trials.
Hoping deeply that this may be
an expiation of sins.

Humans must strive to be optimistic,
believing that there will surely be a happy
ending because of all these very difficult trials.

Allah tests those He loves.
Always rely on Him, place your trust in Him and
constantly work for good.
The happy ending is near, dear sister, in shaa
Allah.

May the Most High make it easy for us.
آمين

You have probably woken up one morning
with that feeling of profound emptiness.
Feeling no emotions, having no desire for
anything, just wanting to sleep, as if life had
lost had its flavor and was no longer worth
living...
In those moments, make sure you cling to
Allah with all your strength.
Let prayer be your refuge, and never stop asking
our Lord to make it easier for you.
It is a temporary feeling that will
completely fade away with time.

So do not be afraid. Everything will eventually
fall into peace, you just need to be patient for a
while...

*May Allah increase your patience and soothe
your little heart.*
آمين

Trials are painful.
They hurt and make you dig deep inside.
When tears keep flowing,
When the heart is broken,
And relief is hoped for,
Allah is there.

Trials are painful, yet trials are
necessary.
Because after them, we will be stronger.
Because after them, we will be wiser.
Because after them, we will be better and do
better.

May the Lord of the worlds grant us a
favorable outcome from our trials.

Fraternally, S.

May the Most Merciful soothe your deepest wounds and turn them into strength for your soul to overcome trials.

آمين

My sweet sister,
As you seek to marry,
Know that it is crucial to choose the right partner.
Choose someone who is best able to listen to you,
understand you, provide for your needs and push
you to the top in every aspect of life.
May this person only wish to help you get closer
to Allah, together walking the path towards
Paradise.

It is important that you choose a man who is
psychologically fit to care for his wife and look
after his household.
A man who is responsible, mature and
serious.
Be aware that marriage is not a game!
Your entire future depends on it, as a home will
be built upon this foundation...

To marry is to completely give yourself to the person who will now share your life.
For us women, the husband is the one who will take on this "religious education", the one we will rely on, the one who will advise us and comfort us.
He will be one of the pillars of our life and our home.

Choose a pious man because if Allah is present in his heart, he will always strive to fulfill his duties towards you, just as you do towards him.

May Allah grant you a pious half who will be a reason for your entry into Paradise.
آمين

Do not give up on marriage, sweet sister.
Perhaps some of the people around have had bad
experiences, it is simply fate and it must be accepted.
Marriage brings countless benefits. Among
them: rest, peace of mind with your partner
and freedom from temptation and
prohibitions.
Take the plunge and fear nothing as long as
you place your trust in Him.
He will make sure you get what is best for you.
Everything that comes from it will be for your
own good. Even if we sometimes do not seem
pleasant, there is always some good in it. Never
doubt that.

May Allah make marriage easy for you.
آمين

For you, my sister-wife,
Difficulties arising during marriage are
completely normal.
When we marry, each one must have the maturity to
recognize that we will overlook our partner's flaws.
At times, it is necessary to accept
misunderstandings, disagreements and differences.
However, it is crucial to focus on the good that
comes from marriage and overlook what is negative.

As long as your partner behaves well most of
the time, be patient and resilient.
Marriage is not a simple matter.
There may be doubts and sometimes even
regrets, but you always end up feeling happy
and grateful.

The perfect marriage does not exist.
All couples go through difficult times.

The most important thing is to come out of it stronger and to be aware that these trials are a blessing to strengthen the bond that unites the lovers, and to feel gratitude to the Lord for having found each other.

May Allah make marriage easy for us and ease our relationships.
آمين

You love being alone, but feeling lonely deeply saddens you.
It is indeed very important to have someone in your life who really listens to you.
Expressing yourself through words is a necessity. Of course, Allah is constantly with us, but human beings are not meant to live eternally alone.

Patience and hope.
One day, He will grant you that person who will be a cause of appeasement in this worldly life.
He will grant you that soul who will make your trials easier by His will.

Entrust yourself completely to Him, and He will fulfill your desires in shaa Allah.

May Allah grant it to you.
آمين

Know that no wound is irreparable. By the will
of the Most Merciful, everything heals, even
the greatest sorrows you have experienced.
Do not lose hope in the healing of your heart
and the mending of your wounds.
Invoke Him.
He listens to you and He will certainly hear
you in shaa Allah.
Some hearts are more sensitive and tested
than others, but all hearts belong to Allah.

How can we not to take care of them?

It is up to you to preserve this precious heart
that He has given you.
Stay away from anything that might hurt you
and turn you into a tormented soul.
Preserve yourself, my sweet sister, as you
would have protected your child from all
harm.

*May Allah guide you on the path of preservation and
keep you away from all harm.*
آمين

Always think positive thoughts and be
optimistic in all circumstances.
It will certainly help better endure life's trials.
After hardship comes ease, my dear. Try to keep
in mind all the moments that make you smile
and that enable you to face life's challenges
better.

Take the time to really appreciate the
moments and the things that bring you joy,
they are so precious...

May Allah keep you away from pessimism.
آمين

Death does not warn, but the Most High has warned us.

What are we waiting for to turn back to

Him? Let us reform our souls while we

still can.

May the Most High grant us the patience
we need to overcome our trials.

آمين

Do not waste your time chasing things that are
not meant for you.
What belongs to you will rightfully come back to you.
Allah is not unjust, and He only loves what is
good for His servant.

How can you not trust Him when He removes
what is bad from your life and replaces it with
something good?

You might not see this good immediately, but
with hindsight and time, you will realize the
wisdom in His decisions.

*It is often said that Allah breaks your heart
to save your soul from a bigger disaster.
SubhanAllah! After all, isn't that wonderful?*

May Allah fill your heart with love and trust in Him.
آمين

Be constantly grateful to your Lord for all the
blessings He bestows upon you.
Some have passed away before they could,
Don't wait until it is too late.
Let the fear ingratitude become a part of
you, it will prevent you from being
ungrateful.
Never stop thanking Him and remember all the
prayers answered by His Grace.

Isn't that extraordinary?

Al hamdulillah

May Allah keep you away from ingratitude.
آمين

You may suffer in silence, far from the eyes
of others, unknown to your loved ones.
But your Lord knows what is in your heart; He
alone knows the extent and depth of your
sadness.
Do not hesitate to entrust yourself to
Him, leave aside the creatures for the
Creator.
He is the One who will bring silence to
the deafening chaos in your heart.
He will not abandon you, do not be afraid.
He is your most faithful company and will
remain so for the rest of your life.

Your heart will find peace by listening to His
gentle words. Replace listening to music
with the Quran, it is a true remedy.

May Allah expiate your sins through your sadness.
آمين

My dear,
I would like to advise you to make sure you
have this constant willingness to learn,
whether religiously or otherwise.
Be curious, nurture your creativity and
intelligence, and become an inspiration in
your own right!
You will feel a little less empty, a bit more
complete.

Do not be afraid to be ambitious as long as
your plans are in accordance with what is
permitted.
Do not let anyone hold you back in your
ambitions and make you believe that progress
is wrong.

I encourage you to pursue your dreams if you
have the ability to do so, and to go beyond your
limits.
Whatever is good for you, your Lord will make
it easy for you.

May Allah help you to achieve this.
آمين

Do not be afraid to part ways with people who bring no benefit into your life.
Those souls that do not bring you any kind of spiritual, psychological, or human benefit should simply no longer accompany you.
Friendships need to be enriching, beneficial and mutual.
Otherwise, solitude becomes safer and the best company.

Make the right choice because your friendships influence you and represent you.

May Allah grant you a quality circle of companions.
آمين

Stop trying to change others. No soul can do so
except for itself.
You can only contribute to that change.
Just as you cannot heal a person but only
contribute to their healing.

Focus on the change you can bring to
yourself.
Accept others as you would like to be
accepted.

May Allah help you to understand this.
آمین

My sweet,
A man who properly cares for his wife, ensuring her well-being, meeting her needs, listening to her, and advising her, is not a myth.

You just need for a pious man who truly fears his Lord and desires the best for his household.
Thus, if the foundation of your relationship is religion, it can only be beneficial for both of you.
Each will strive for the other to fulfillment and will do everything to ensure the spouse's satisfaction in order to be reunited in Paradise.

Al hamdulillah, what a ni'ma isn't it?

However, what will happen next is a matter of destiny, and you can be sure that your Lord's decision is always the best one.

May Allah grant you a pious husband who will take care of you.
آمين

My precious sister,
I sincerely hope that you will experience
true love, the kind that comes from a fully
halal relationship.
Do not lose patience, your other half will
eventually show up, sometimes when you
least expect it, which will certainly surprise
you.
I wish you every success with this union that
complete half of your religion.
So do not rush off, my sweet,
Soulmates eventually find each other
when they know how to wait.

صبر

*May Allah make this union a source of complete
happiness.*
آمين

Do not let anyone come between you and your Lord.
If there is one relationship that needs to be preserved, it is this one.

How can you allow someone to take you away from the One who rules your heart?

Do not be afraid to leave relationships that distance you from Him or prevent you from getting closer to Him.
This is by no means a loss because the souls sincerely wishing for your happiness will only guide you towards Him.

You are bound to be tested by this in the course of your life but stay strong.
Your Lord comes first.

May Allah help you to stay away from bad people.
آمين

My sweet,
Do not be afraid of failure.
Your goals will take the time they need to
materialize.
What is important is that you persevere
with patience and optimism.
Do not dwell on a thousand questions; just go for it.
Action is necessary to pursue your dreams.
You will get there with the help of Allah in
shaa Allah. He is the indispensable support
you need,
you do not need anyone else's approval to
pursue your dreams.

*May the Almighty grant all your wishes if they are
good for you.*
آمين

My sweet ukht,
Ensure you constantly care for the pearl that
you are, for even diamonds need to be
cherished.
Do not wait until you are at your limit to
start; that would be a big mistake.

Do not silence your emotions and what your
body wants to tell you.
Take the time to listen to what is going on inside you.
Take the time to take a break and refocus on
yourself.
Take the time to cut yourself off from the world
and recharge your batteries.
Do not neglect yourself.
You are primarily responsible for your own
physical and psychological well-being.

May Allah take care of you.
آمين

Oh, my hypersensitive sister,
Sometimes you feel as if everything is falling
apart around you when the emotion seems
intense and overwhelming.
Do not be disoriented by this, keep working on
yourself and eventually, you will succeed in
controlling your reactions.

Do not listen to those who claim you are
"abnormal", because you are not.
Your difference will always be a great and
honorable quality, but above all a strength.
Your hypersensitivity is not your weakness, no
matter what other people think.
It is a gift from your Lord that will bring you
beautiful surprises in your life.
It is up to you to change this negative view
and emerge stronger than ever.

May Allah make it easy for you.
آمين

Do not waste your time on trivial matters
because time keeps running out.
Every day that your Lord makes may be the
last, so do not waste what is left of your life on
things that aren't worth it.
Be aware of the chance He gives you to live one
more day.
One more day to praise and worship Him.
One more morning, one more day, one more
evening to cherish the presence of the souls
you hold dear.
Repent to Him and never tire of seeking His
forgiveness.
Indeed, your return will be to Him.

*May Allah grant us the awareness of the
preciousness of time.*
آمين

My dear,
Entering into an illicit love relationship
thinking it will lead to a certain happiness is
nothing but an illusion on the part of the
sheytan to lead you towards the destruction
of your heart.

*How many hearts have ended up broken as a
result of such relationship? The count is
countless.*

When your Lord forbids you to do something,
it is because it holds harmful for you.
Your soulmate will find you at the right time,
do not rush.
Hearts meant to be together, Allah
will bring them together.
All you need to do is trust your Creator and be
patient for as long as it takes.
What is meant for you will come to you, do not
doubt it.

*May Allah grant you the necessary patience and
may He reunite you.*
آمين

Do not let mental ruminations slowly consume you, turning you into a mere shadow of yourself.

No matter regrets or remorse haunting you, choose to entrust yourself to your Lord and empty your heart of all these negatives thoughts.
He is The Only One capable of appeasing you.
However, you must put your trust in Him and take steps so that He can help you.
You have to believe in Him, in His abilities, His power.
All He wants is for you to draw closer to Him through this trial.
Do not let the sheytan darken your thoughts and make you despair of the Mercy of your Creator.
By having Allah in your life, by being grateful for this chance to have Him, deliverance will not be long in coming.

May Allah make you a completely fulfilled and serene woman.
آمين

Sometimes you get the feeling that your
existence is meaningless, that living is
synonymous with misery and sadness.
You might have even attempted to end your
life because the pain was unbearable.
Tears seem to have lost their purpose for you,
crying has become a daily habit.
You feel weak, powerless, helpless,
misunderstood, but above all, very alone.

*Know that Allah does not burden a soul
beyond that it can bear.
Do you know what that means?*

It means you are a fighter, a strong woman.
Do not forget that you have the best weapon to
fight and combat these negative thoughts.
Your weapon is your faith. It is Islam.
 Allah is with you, my sister.

Allah has not abandoned you. He is the only One
who will never let you down.
You will never be alone, because He is always
with you.
He listens to you, He knows what lies in your
heart, and He only waits for one thing: for you
to turn to Him.

Your life is not meaningless, my dear.
You were created to worship your Lord.
Focus on this task and leave behind anything
that brings you sadness.
Distance yourself from anything that causes
you pain, toxicity, or harm to your soul.

Do not be afraid to give up the things that
cause you despair and anything that does
not benefit you.
Be kind to yourself and take care of the heart
that your Lord has given you.

Now that you know that you are not alone, that
He understands you and loves you, it is your turn
to love Him in return.
All the pain you are feeling will gradually
disappear with time.
Courage, my sister, it is only a matter of time
before your soul unburdens itself.

*May Allah purify your heart, bring you closer to Him
and keep you away from anything harmful.*
آمين

Do not let the pain of the past and the fear of
the future paralyze your present.

What matters is the present moment.
You cannot act outside of that moment.
Your Lord will comfort you.

It is up to you to make sure you take the
right decisions so that past mistakes do not
happen again.

Your future depends on your present, and you
need to focus all your energy on the present
moment.
And Don't worry, your Lord is with you,
supporting you, and will never abandon you.

May Allah ease your pains and apprehensions.
آمین

We often do everything in our power to save
our relationships.
We give our all, make every necessary effort, but
it is still not enough.
At that precise moment, it is crucial to accept
the situation to avoid prolonging the
inevitable.
When it is the end of a relationship, nothing can
change that, it is qadar Allah.

Do not be distressed.
Persistence and insistence are not really
appropriate in this situation.
It is like exhausting yourself for a lost cause.

If a relationship is meant to end, there is a good
reason behind it, despite all the pain it will cause
you.
You will feel sad, sometimes nostalgic, but try to
remember only the good times so that the
memory of that relationship remains pleasant.
Never forget that Allah wants nothing but your
happiness. All His decisions are for your well-
being.

*May Allah ease our separation from His
creatures.*
آمين

My sweet,
Strive to be more of an attentive ear than a
talkative mouth.
Our relationships are often too selfish.
We talk more than we listen.
Each of us has the ability to help improve
someone's psychological well-being.
A few words are all it takes for a semblance of
happiness when our whole world is falling apart.
A compliment, a kind word…
Show yourself tender, kind, gentle and
pleasant – it is contagious. Others will
reciprocate with the same kindness towards
you.

And above all, do not forget to smile. It never hurt
anyone and it is even a Sunnah!

*May Allah soften our relations with our loved ones
and bring us closer to them.*
آمين

To you, my sweetheart wishing to marry,
The wait seems endless and the time so long.
Your Lord surely has a plan for you.
Everything happens at the right time and the
best things take time.
Do not despair and put your trust in
Him.
Deliverance is certainly near.

Do not worry about how long it might take,
because there is no age limit for getting married.
It will take as long as it takes, and when it does,
you will fully enjoy this long-awaited moment.
Fear not. Your soulmate, the one who will
complement your faith, has already been
written for you.
What is destined for you will come to you
rightfully.
Be patient and pray to your Creator to bring you
together.

*Soulmates eventually find each other when
they learn to wait, Don't they?*

May Allah ease your wait and bring you together.
آمين

Your soul is just a traveler in this ephemeral world.
Your corporeal envelope is meant to return
to its Creator.

Are you ready to join Him?

Because death does not wait, it will come
whether you are ready for it or not.
Prepare your grave, no soul will carry your
deeds for you.

*You will have to answer for them, are
you aware?*

Do not wait until it is too late to enjoin good
and forbid evil.
It is said that this world is a prison for the
believer and a paradise for the disbeliever.

On which side do you stand?

*May the Most Merciful guide you towards the right
choices that bring you closer to Him.*
آمين

No trial is insurmountable,
your Lord will never burden you beyond what
you can bear.

Your life will continue to be filled with
challenges to bring you closer to Him.
Every trial you encounter is meant to draw you
nearer to Him.
Do not hate Him, for His sole purpose is to have
His creatures in Paradise.

Believers will continually be tested in order to
earn Firdaws, how can you achieve this merit
without proving yourself?

Hold on to Him, and hope for a happy ending with your
loved ones in the Gardens of Eden.

May the Creator of the worlds grant you His Paradise.
آمين

Sweet soul,
Relief will surely come just as you are about to
surrender.
It is a matter of waiting a few more moments.
Rest is just around the corner.
Your endurance will turn into satisfaction.
Do not lose heart, do not give up; your Lord
sees you and He will deliver you.
Your patience can only be beneficial.
It strengthens your soul and prepares it for
the next challenges.
After the hardship comes ease.
You will come out stronger.

*May the Clement One give you the patience needed
to overcome your trials.*
آمين

When life exhausts you, remember Allah. Your
heart will be relieved by listening to His words.
Your soul belongs to Him; relieve it by
nourishing it with His reminder.
The exhaustion will gradually wear off.
Do not forget that the purpose of this worldly life
here below is not happiness and fun.
It's a test you have to pass to earn your place
in the Garden of Delights.
Piety will bring serenity and rest to your
heart.
Draw close to Him and He will make it easy for you.

May the Omnipotent relieve your heart at His reminder.
آمين

Do not let yourself be discouraged by the
weight of your sins. The darkness may
continue to attract you.
Remember, He is the Infinitely Merciful and
Forgiving.
Repent to Him in this life by correcting
your path.
Do not let yourself weaken by your inner
struggle. Your soul will surely return to its
Creator.
Make your steps a direction towards His
light.
Be patient, as our pious predecessors were
patient.

Perseverance will be the key to your happiness.

*May the Lord of the Worlds facilitate your
jihad an-nafs.*
آمين

May the Most High make us pious, tender, gentle, and loving women.
آمین

O sweet sister,
You are a woman, a mother, a daughter, a
wife.
You are gentle, kind, loving and caring.
Yet, you are also brave and strong.
You bear and give life.
You educate. You are the pillar of your family.
Do not let anyone diminish your status and
role as a woman.
Islam regards you as a pearl that must be
respected and preserved.

May the All-Knowing One love you.
آمين

Do not worry about what people think of you.
We cannot please everyone; humans constantly
change.
Focus instead on what your Lord thinks of
you. It is Him you must satisfy.
He is the only One who can change your
circumstances in this worldly life.
He is the only One who forgives all your
wrongdoings, as long as you sincerely repent to
him. Detach yourself from others to draw closer
to Him. It is up to you not to neglect Him.
You must make Him your priority.

*May the Most High detach your heart from this
fleeting life.*
آمين

Protect your heart from anything that
could harm it.
Be cautious not to endanger it or expose
its weaknesses to the world.
Do not run towards your destruction.
Distance it from relationships that do not benefit
it and cause deep suffering.
Be for your heart a mother who will keep it away
from all evils.
Who will never let it fall for the sake of others.
And Don't forget to feed him with the remembrance
of Allah.
Fill your heart with love for Him and His

messenger ﷺ.

He is the One who will purify it when
you ask Him to.
Your heart belongs to Him, so take care of
it...

*May the Creator of all things keep your heart away
from harm.*
آمين

Do not wait for happiness to embrace you in
this worldly life.
The goal is not to be happy here, but in
Paradise.
Your existence is only ephemeral; you have
been created solely to worship Him.
You will face trials to prove your
submission and devotion to Him.
Prepare for the worst to savor the best.

After hardship comes ease, al hamduliLlah
for everything and despite everything.

صبر

May the Most High make your trials an expiation of
sins and bring you closer to Him.
آمين

Behind every hardship lies some good.
Your Lord knows what you do not
know.
You may have been broken, disappointed or
betrayed, finding yourself locked in sadness,
forgetting that your Lord was nearby.

Then one beautiful day, you realized that your
trials were not entirely in vain but were in fact
beneficial.
You learned, you understood, and you
grew.
You are still here, stronger than ever,
because Allah will never burden you with
more than you can handle.

Trust Him.
Everything you go through is temporary.
Your final destination is with Him, hopefully in
His Paradise.
Always keep in mind this hoped-for end and the
fact that He will soothe all your pains, for Your
Lord loves you.

*May the Most Merciful keep you away from despair
and fill your heart with His Light and Love.*
آمين

Never underestimate the power of gentleness.

How many hearts have been soothed and reassured by it? Countless.

Train your soul to be gentle. But above all, be gentle with yourself so that you can be gentle with others.
And do not heed those who would discourage you from it. It is a quality that can only foster love and brotherhood.

Al hamduliLlah

May the Lord grant you the sweetness of honey.
آمين

Remember that everything is ephemeral so
that peace reigns in your heart.
Detach yourself from this worldly life to
refocus on your meeting with your Lord in
the hereafter.
Your eternal home is with Him, and all the
ties that bind you here will eventually fade.
So do not worry about material possessions.
What matters is your spiritual elevation.
I hope the end will be happy for you,
Put everything in motion to ensure that it is.

*May the Forgiver detach your heart from this
worldly life.*
آمين

Allah has not made you sad for no reason.
He knows what you do not. His decisions are
only good for you.
The more patient you are, the greater the
reward, such is His promise.
Take this opportunity to thank Him for not
forgetting you.
He loves you and will always be there to watch
over you.
Put your trust in Him, deliverance can only be
near.

*May the Holder of souls relieve your sadness
and expiate your sins through it.*
آمين

Do not regret having met certain
people in your life.
Every encounter brings something,
whether good or bad.
Happiness or a lesson.
Experiences are only beneficial.
Time and distance will make you understand this.

Be patient...

*May the Most High bring you closer to
people who are good for your soul.*
آمين

Time goes by so quickly...
You do not have time to hate or slander.
Focus on your relationship with your Lord.
Make sure you do not feel any remorse or regret.
Make the most of the time you have left to sow
goodness so that you can find it when you need it
most.
Be a source of happiness and joy for yourself and
others.
Remember to nurture your relationship
with your loved ones and to love with all
your heart.

*May the Wise One grant you reflection on the
benefits of using your time wisely.*
آمين

Silence and ignoring trivialities will allow your soul to reach tranquility.

Detach yourself from what others may think and say about you.
Ignore anything that harms your psychological well-being.
Keep your tongue away from complaining and gossiping.
Let silence prevail at times when words are reprehensible.
Be mindful that your Lord sees you, hears you and knows what lies deep within you.
Concern yourself with the fate that awaits you on the day when all souls will be reunited before Him.
What matters is to escape Hell and find yourself in Paradise.

May the Most Merciful detach your heart from the trivialities of this worldly life.
آمين

Do not listen to those who say silence is a
weakness.
They fail to recognize that it demonstrates
intelligence and wisdom.
Be proud to master that piece of flesh that is
your tongue, for it is a piece of flesh that could
lead many to Hell.
Never tire of silence.
It may well be a companion that leads to your
presence in Paradise.

*May the All-Seeing make silence sweet
company.*
آمين

Stay away from anything that poses a
threat to your religion, values, and dignity.
Whether it is people, situations, or specific
places.
No one else will do it for you, it is up to you
to preserve yourself.
Take care of the soul that your Creator has
entrusted to you.
Do not be your own tormenter by heading
towards what will cause you pain and sadness.
Never stop invoking Him.
He is the only One who can keep you
away from those who would harm you.

*May the Most High grant you the understanding of
the preservation of your soul.*
آمين

Love with all your heart as much as
possible, while staying reasonable.
Do not let bad experiences deprive you of loving
and being loved.
Every wound has a beneficial aspect.
Your Lord only wants what is good for
you.
Trust Him.
He distances you away from that which
separates you from Him and draws you
closer to that which brings you closer to
Him.
Living without love is hardly possible,
Do not try to reject this feeling, which is a
source of happiness and integrity.
Open yourself to love.
This life is too short to walk away from it.

*May the Most Dominant protect you from everything
that may hurt your heart.*
آمين

When your Lord sends you signs to discern the
true intentions of others, do not ignore them.

Some hide behind a false face to charm and win
you over.
Others take advantage of your carefree
nature and naivety to manipulate you.
Be aware of what He wants to show you.
He is the only one who knows what hearts
conceal and the deep intentions of His
creatures.

Show wisdom and maturity by distancing
yourself from what is harmful to you, even if it
means a difficult separation.

*May the All-Merciful preserve you from those with ill
intentions.*
آمين

The eye weeps when the soul suffers.
You may feel lonely and helpless in the face of
this suffering.
Words cannot describe the pain that haunts
you.
Know that in this trial, your Lord has neither
forsaken you nor abandoned you.
He tests you because He loves you.
Repent and call upon Him so that this sadness
may serve as an expiation for your sins.

*May the Most Merciful draw you closer to Him
through this sadness.*
آمين

Even if everyone leaves you, Allah is enough for you.

Take care to keep Him in your life.
He is the One who is truly concerned about you.
Your happiness and sustenance depend on Him
alone.
To completely rely on Allah means not fearing
anything, because we know that He takes the
best decisions, even if we cannot see His plan...
Remember that your soul is destined to return to
your Lord.
So, your existence, along with our joys
and sorrows, is temporary.

Therefore, do not worry, try to remember Him
constantly so that He does not forget you.

May the Greatest never cease to bring you closer to Him.
آمين

May the Most Merciful bring calm to your mind so that your soul may find peace.
آمین

Your smile is the wealth that no human being
can take away from you.
The choice is yours.
It may be that certain people, or certain trials
take away your desire to shine,
but the decision is yours.
Do not let anyone force you to do anything about it.

*Smiling is a Sunnah, but it's also an act of
charity. Why deprive yourself of it?*

*May Allah grant you a beautiful smile that you will
never tire of.*
آمين

Do not let your heart be attached to what is not
allowed.
Once you find yourself in chaos and
temptation, distance yourself to avoid falling
into what is forbidden.
A haram relationship will only bring you pain.
The sheytan may lead you to the illusion
of perfect happiness, but sooner or later,
reality will catch up, and it will be quite
the opposite.
You will only regret letting yourself be
influenced.

Be strong and never stop moving away from the
forbidden, constantly calling upon your Lord to
strengthen your faith.

May your Lord keep you away from all prohibitions.
آمين

Are you looking for love, hope and peace?

Choose Allah! He is what you seek.
He will fulfill your needs, for your soul
belongs to Him.
He is the One who will never betray or
disappoint you.
Choose Him.
Loneliness will abandon your heart, because
from now on, He is with you wherever you
are.

*May the Lord of the worlds fill your heart
with love for him.*
آمین

Beautiful souls always respond to the harm
they receive with kindness.
Such is the gentle soul; it does not let the
cruelty of others darken it

Is that the case for you?

It is never too late to soften your soul by
purifying your heart.
The love you might not have received, pass it
on. It will undoubtedly fill that deep void-within
you.

May the Most High make your soul a haven of peace.
آمين

Strive to be optimistic.
It is not about having an utopian or naive vision
of life.
It is about placing your trust in Allah,
for behind every hardship lies a blessing.
Place your trust in your Lord!
Be positive and optimistic!
An optimistic outlook will be much more
beneficial than a pessimistic view of life
and the things that may happen to you.

With effort, it is possible!
Invoke Him and He will make it easier for you.

May the Most High keep you away from pessimism.
آمين

Whatever disagreements you may have had with
your loved ones, do your best to restore the
bonds that unite you.
Do not let the affairs of this world keep you
away from those who have repeatedly
shown their attachment and love for you.
Put aside pride and ego, they are not good
advisors.
It often takes very little to restore peace among
you.

As time goes by, make sure you make the right
choices, so you do not have any regrets.

*May the Lord of the Worlds restore peace in your
relationships.*
آمين

And even if you feel like you're losing track of
life, do not worry.
Your Lord is The One who manages everything
perfectly.
Do not worry, He is watching over you as long as
you do not forget Him and place your trust in Him.

May the Most High bring peace to your heart.
آمين

You feel like the pain will never go away
because the memories keep flooding in.

That is the source of your despair.

The wounds are healable,
because Allah is the Healer of hearts.
The soul finds comfort in listening to His
words and evoking Him.

What are you waiting for to start?

Do not let the dips in faith distance you from
Him or make you believe that misfortune
awaits you.
He is indeed the One who wishes no harm to
His servant. So, rely on Him.
Your heart will gradually heal from all the
inflicted pains.
Trust Him, all pain is only temporary.

*May Allah ease your deepest suffering and allow
you to emerge stronger.*
آمين

We often tend to neglect our relationships.
We would like to be treated properly, with
respect, sincerity, and courtesy.

What about our own behavior?

Let us start by behaving in the same way we
would like to be treated.
Reciprocity will gradually occur...
Lies and oppression will leave our relationships,
and love will grow even more.
Let us not wait for bitterness to take shape, let
us look after each other.

*May the Most High allow us to bring peace to our
hearts.*
آمين

Do you know that Allah only made you sad to make you happy?

He never saddens you without a reason.
There is always good hidden behind all these trials and tears...
The most difficult trials you have experienced are not meant to destroy you,
but are intended to strengthen your faith.
Realize that He is testing you to bring you closer to Him.
Your Lord loves you, never doubt it or forget it.

May the Most High transform your sadness into immense joy.
آمين

As believers, we must accept our Destiny, whether it is good or bad, happy or sad, easy or difficult.
Everything that results from our lives corresponds to His decision, the most just possible.

He is the One in whom we must place our complete trust and devotion.
He is the holder of our soul, the One who grants us breath.
No soul will be able to turn away from Him on the Last Day.

How is it possible to want to escape Him?

Do not worry, O gentle soul!
This life is nothing but ephemeral. All your worries are only temporary. Struggling in this world is necessary to earn your place in Paradise.
Accept His decree, and your existence will be easier to overcome.

May the Greatest facilitate your acceptance of His decree.
آمين

Be proud of the generosity of your heart
and the purity of your soul.

The love, time, and consideration you have
offered throughout your life will never be in vain.
All relationships certainly have a beneficial
aspect, regardless of the sadness they may have
caused. Do not let regrets overwhelm you and
prevent you from loving again.

*Life would have a completely different taste
without love, don't you think?*

*May the Most Merciful purify your heart and
keep you away from evil people.*
آمين

Throughout your existence, you will be faced
with numerous temptations.
The sheytan will not cease to try to divert you
from the purpose of your existence, which is to
worship your Creator. The forbidden will appear
attractive and easily accessible.
He will tempt you to break His laws, even if only
for a moment.

Do not let yourself be fooled, because when
haram is committed, the illusion of its beauty
will vanish and your heart, filled with regret, will
never stop weeping.
When this happens, sincerely repent to Him.
He will forgive you because He is The
Most Merciful, so do not despair.

*May the Most Merciful keep you away from the
temptations of this world and strengthen your faith.*
آمين

Do you know that the final return will be to Him?

Why then do you behave as if your soul were
self-sufficient?
It needs the One to whom it belongs, Allah.
This soul that should only strive to worship and
praise Him.
Your role is to educate it so that it relies
only on Him.

*So, what about its use? Have you
respected what your Lord has taught you?*

Do not stop meditating, for the time flies by and
your existence is not eternal.
The day when you will be held accountable
to Him is certainly approaching very fast.

May the Most High facilitate for you jihad an-nafs.
آمين

You spend your days constantly
surrounded or occupied, trying to escape
the troubles that weigh on your life.
But when night falls, you find yourself alone
in bed.

Negative thoughts cloud your mind, despite
your efforts to evade them.
Then you realize that avoidance is merely a
temporary fix.

The true remedy lies in facing the problems
head-on and accepting what has transpired.

Suddenly, you come to understand that you
are not truly alone, for Allah will never
abandon you. Everything that happens to you
is by His decree, and He only seeks your well-
being.

So, you decide to draw closer to Him.
Gradually, the bad thoughts leave your nights
to make way for peace of mind.
All off this is thanks to Him.

Be grateful and strive never to forget Him,
praising Him throughout your life.

May Allah preserve you, sweetheart.
آمين

Some people are truly meant to stay in our hearts, but not in our lives.
If Allah has ordained it so, then undoubtedly there is no good in it.
Let us put our trust in Him.
Separations are certainly painful, but or will only last for a while.
Instead of lamenting, thank Him for taking you away from those who take you away from Him.
He loves you, thus He preserves you.

May Allah soothe your heart from painful separations.
آمين

It is difficult to detach from relationships that
are not beneficial.
We cling to the nostalgia of the person's
former self.
Although the change no longer aligns with
our lifestyles, we refuse to accept that this
change is permanent.
So, we hold on to an outdated reality that we
struggle to let go of.

We keep hoping that this person will revert
to who they once were, which is hard to accept.
Reality eludes us and nostalgia dominates us.

Allah has probably shown you signs so that you
understand that you need to end certain
relationships.
So, do not ignore them and do not distress.
Place your trust in Him and resume your life by
placing your hopes only in Him.

*May the Lord erase this nostalgia that is
preventing you from living.*
آمين

The heart is truly saddened when it loves
deeply but has to leave this companionship
because love is no longer enough.
Reason emerges when respect and
consideration have left the relationship.
The heart can only heed reason,
for listening to reason is protecting the heart.

Your Lord has given you life to worship Him.
Do not let the things of this world distract
you from your goal and force you to abandon
it.

Do not love beyond your capacity, for He is the
only One who deserves all your love and
devotion.

May the Most Merciful keep your heart away
from harmful and toxic loves.
آمين

By the will of Allah,
Souls destined to unite cannot miss each other.
Even if the whole world tries to separate
them, they will continue to find each other.
Only a few moments of patience separate you
from meeting your other half.
Your Lord has bound your souls for a good
reason, probably for eternity.
So, place your trust in Him, your soulmate will
be yours at the right time.
Preserve yourself while waiting to welcome him
in the best possible way.

*May the Lord of the Worlds unite your souls and
make love reign between you.*
آمين

Two souls who love each other for the sake of Allah and bind themselves before Him can only hope to reunite in Paradise.

And what better destination than His Garden of Delights, in the company of the beloved?

The foundation of the relationship, which is nothing but piety, can only lead them to this coveted place.
The closer the couple is to Allah, the closer they will be to each other.
The love will only intensify and strengthen.

Are you ready to strive never to part?

May Allah bless your marriage and grant you His vast Paradise.
آمين

May Allah grant us a righteous spouse and
righteous offspring.
آمين

Do not be among those who steal the joy of
others, who darken someone's heart,
or who constrain someone's goodness.
Instead, be among those who bring back
smiles when everything seems bleak and
contribute to the blossoming of souls and
the soothing of hearts.

When death calls upon us,
Each one hope to receive invocations from
those they knew in their lifetime, so that
their trials may be eased.
There is never too much time to rejoice the
hearts of those we love.
Let us deeply cherish the time we have left
before He calls us back to Him.

*May the Lord make love and peace reign in our
hearts and keep us away from all evil and harmful
things.*
آمين

I pray to Allah that the reservoir of love He
offers us never runs dry.
May He allow us to love Him and everything that
brings us closer to Him.
May He grant us the ability to love
throughout our lives without ever growing
weary.
May He enable us to love without ever
losing hope.
May He make us a source of peace through our
love for our beloved.
May He allow us to accept the love of
others without doubt.

May He allow our love to endure in the hearts of
those we love beyond life. May death never put
an end to the affection and tenderness we feel.

*May Allah allow us to reunite in Paradise so that we
continue to cherish and love each other.*
آمين

My dear,
Be the strong and honorable woman you want
your daughter to be.
Do not cease to nurture tenderness and kindness
so that your heart never tires of shining.
Do not go for anything that might
diminish your worth and your dignity.
You are the mistress of your home.
What a noble status and beautiful
responsibility!
Therefore, do not forget to preserve your
mental health to avoid breaking down.
You are the role model for your little ones.
Reflect the image you would like them to embody.

*What better example for a son than his
mother, so that he knows what kind of woman
to marry?*

*What better example for the daughter than her
mother, so she knows what kind of behavior to
adopt?*

*May the Most High make you a fulfilled woman and
mother, and may He ease the fulfillment of your duties
and responsibilities*
آمين

The sweetness and kindness you exhibit are
extremely honorable and commendable
qualities.

Do not let anyone rob you of your desire to
spread kindness.
The tenderness that emanates from you
will only enhance your beauty.

They will never stop trying to destroy the good
in you so that you become like them.
You will certainly not take revenge, for your
Lord will take care of that.

And what better support than Him?

May the One who holds your soul protect you
from the malice of some.
آمين

Peace be upon those who transmit kindness
and goodness despite all the harm done to
them.

آمين

We ask the Most High that solitude be a peace to your soul and a comfort to your heart.

آمين

Among the deep sorrows felt by solitary souls is
the longing to share so much, yet having no
company to confide in.
Indeed, solace for these souls is found in
Islam.
Allah hears and sees everything perfectly.

The secret battles they wage are known only to
their Creator, which brings some comfort to
their hearts.
Solitary souls are those who know themselves
best and appreciate themselves most.
They tolerate no bad company, preferring
solitude over it.

*The quest for beneficial companionship has been
very challenging for them, so they have isolated
themselves to draw closer to their Lord in peace
and tranquility.*

*May the Most High grant you the company of
beneficial souls, so that together you may
advance towards Him.*
آمين

Be patient, even if your heart twists in pain and
overflows with sadness.
Remember that Allah's promise is true.
He will continue to test those He loves.
Behind every long patience lies a huge reward.
Trust Him, beautiful things are worth the
wait.

Patience brings many blessings, teaching
your soul resilience and endurance.
So never lose heart in waiting and seeking
His guidance.
It will surely bring solace to your heart.

*What a wonderful virtue patience is, and
what a magnificent gift Your Lord has given
you, don't you think?*

*May the Almighty reward you abundantly for
your unwavering trust in Him.*
آمين

Wish healing to those who have caused you pain
and peace to those who wanted to break you.
The pain they spread within you will surely
return to them, for Your Lord never fails His
promise.
No injustice will go unpunished.

Live up to His expectations.
Forget vengeance, which will lead your soul to
repeat the wrongs they committed.
You are worth so much more than that.
Besides, holding a grudge will only intensify
the sadness deep inside you.

Allah will undoubtedly soothe your heart, as
long as you place your complete trust in Him.
He is the One who always fulfills His
promises.
Put your trust in Him, for He will never forsake you.

*May the All-Knowing allow you to repay evil with
kindness to elevate your soul.*
آمين

Your Lord may be testing you, for He desires Paradise for you. What more could you wish for?

This earthly abode is certainly not a life of rewards, but of trials.
Thus, every trial we overcome inevitably brings us something beneficial for the future.
Every hardship that arises from trials always leaves a gift.
Perhaps invisible at first, but with time and perspective, we realize the blessings they bring.

So, do not expect to feel joy in this worldly life, for what matters is that you experience it in the Hereafter.

May the Lord turn every trial into a step towards Paradise.
آمين

Dear solitary soul,
When loneliness feels heavy and overwhelming,
remind your soul that Allah is the One who will
never abandon us.

Solitude makes us realize that we are
absolutely nothing without Allah.
He is the only One on we can rely on
eternally, without any doubt.
Solitude is a real comfort for the heart because
it allows you to meditate and draw closer to
your Creator.

And if you feel like no one understands you,
remember that your Lord knows what is in your
heart.
One day, He will grant you the completeness of
your soul.
Someone who will strive to understand what is
happening within you.

*Do not despair, He will grant you what you
desperately need.*

May Allah turn your solitude into a great blessing.
آمين

How can we truly appreciate moments of joy without experiencing a few moments of sadness?

Sometimes, it is necessary to accept that sadness is part of us in order to better understand the trials of life.
Thus, the sufferings to come will probably seem less unbearable to live, easier to accept.
Use this sadness to enjoy the moments of joy more fully and to be constantly grateful for what your Lord grants you.

And do not forget that He only makes you sad to make you even happier.

May the Most High turn your sadness into a blossoming of your soul.
آمين

Pray to your Lord to bring beauty to your soul
and your heart.
From this beauty of the soul, good behaviour
will blossom, which will probably keep you
away from His burning fire.
Let your tongue speak only sweet and beneficial
words so that it may be good for you on the Day
of Judgment.

Be different from others, dear sister.
Use your behavior to surpass them in goodness and
to elevate yourself in ranks.

May the Omniscient grant you a beautiful soul
that will satisfy Him.
آمين

I pray to Allah that He does not let our hearts
become attached to what is not meant for
them.
May He make it easier for our souls to accept
their destiny and find rest and tranquility.
I pray to Allah that He may bring our hearts
closer to what is lawful and beneficial.
May He prevent us from denying His signs so
that we may abandon what is not permitted.
May He enable us to abandon the things of this
worldly life and cling to the hereafter.

Do not doubt His decisions, for they are only for
our good.

May the Greatest keep us connected to His path.
آمين

When the pain seems unbearable to
overcome, you may think that the Most High is
afflicting you.
Eventually, you realize that all He has only
saved you from affliction.
So, put all your trust in Him.
Double your efforts in seeking forgiveness for all
the times you have doubted His intentions.

You will soon realize that He is the only One
who unquestionably wishes nothing but good
for the believers.
Therefore, believe firmly in Him, for His
generosity is infinite towards those He loves.

*May the Lord of the Universe grant you eternal trust
in Him.*
آمين

Speak to your heart and let it know that
sadness is only fleeting and temporary.
Tell it that the extent of his suffering will be
erased by the will of its Lord.
Assure it that joy will embrace it at the right
moment, probably when it least expects it.

*It may be that the sadness you feel here on
earth is a cause of your happiness in the
hereafter.
And what better life could there be?*

Speak to your heart and tell it that you are
there for it, but that Allah is there for it even
more so.
As long as it clings to Him, it has nothing to
fear.

*May the Lord of the Universe bring joy to your
heart.*
آمين

People are constantly searching for the soul
that can truly complete them, as no one
wishes to remain alone forever.
There is a longing to find someone who
prioritizes spiritual elevation towards Allah
over worldly pursuits.
Such a companion, committed to ascending
to the Most High, becomes a pillar of support
in staying on the right path.

This companion becomes a source of comfort in
times of difficulty and turmoil.
The ultimate aspiration is to reunite in Paradise
and continue the bond of love for eternity.

Isn't that what true love is all about?

*May the Almighty unite those souls destined for
eternal love*
آمين

Do not let your heart drift towards sadness
and regrets.
Entrust yourself to the One who carries the
burden of your soul, for He alone can provide
relief.
Do not let your heart be devoid of hope.
This struggle is merely a means for it to blossom
and ascend.

Keep fighting and you will attain the
peace you have been hoping for.
Joy will gradually find its way into you.
Then you will be proud of enduring and
persevering.

May the Lord grant you endurance and patience.
آمین

The darkness of others may seek to conquer
your heart and corrupt your soul.
Their malevolent whispers are nothing but a
source of sadness and misfortune.
Never tire of fighting them so that your
ultimate destination may be Paradise.

**Do you wish for your soul eternal
rest?**

Then forsake the company of the wicked to
draw closer to Him.
Thus, you may hope for eternal peace of mind
and spirit.

*May Allah keep you away from harmful company
and intrusive thoughts.*
آمين

Do you nourish your heart with the remembrance of its Creator?

The heart cannot remain healthy if it is not attached to the divine words.
Tranquility and serenity cannot dwell in it if it distances itself from the One who created it.
Your duty is to take care of this organ, which will bear witness to your intentions on the Last Day.

Hasten to purify your heart and soul before it is too late...

May the Most Great strengthen your heart in His religion.
آمين

Be a source of comfort around you, a soul that spreads love and joy.
Be a haven of peace for tormented hearts, a soul that provides ease in the difficult of wounded beings.
And do not forget, you may be a lighthouse in someone else's storm...

Do not we all deserve to feel loved and reassured?

May Allah make you a source of comfort for others to elevate you in ranks.
آمین

When you are about to commit a sin, remember that your Lord is constantly watching you.

Is this sin worth committing?

Is it worth distancing yourself from the One who created you, hindering your soul from attaining purity, and corrupting your faith...

Your duty is to preserve this relationship with your Creator and avoid disappointing Him so that He may be satisfied with you.

May the Most High help you to educate your heart and soul.

آمين

He is the One who saves your heart from ruin
and your soul from depravity.
He is the One who guides your heart to truth,
steering your soul away from perdition.
He is the One who grants you ease in
difficulty, restoring your motivation and hope.

Who is He?

Allah.

*May He make you aware of the precious
value of our noble religion.*
آمين

Let the warmth of Allah penetrate your heart.
Your soul can only overflow with tears of joy
and fervor.

He is the One who will fill the deep void
that slumbers within you.
The emptiness will vanish, for He will
replace it with what is better for you.
He will turn your sorrows into an ocean of
love, lessons, and wisdom.

So put your trust in Him.
Open your heart to Him, confide your distress to Him.

*May Al Wadud turn your sorrows into
beneficial lessons of wisdom for your heart.*
آمين

Do not let your heart drift away.
Do not let your soul wither.
You must take care of these treasures that
your Lord has bestowed upon you.
Prevent them from drowning in
depression and anxiety.
So do not let your inner struggle hinder
you from the desired peace.
Invoke Him so that He may ease your way,
He will help you overcome all that pains and
saddens you.

*May the Most High grant you peace of heart
and blossoming of the soul.*
آمين

Do not blame your heart for its purity and
naivety.
It deserves to feel no regret for all the good it
has done.
You can only be proud to have a heart full of
principles and values.
Of course, you will sometimes be saddened by
the lack of recognition and reciprocity.

*But is there a better reward than that
promised by Allah?*

Remember that your actions are only meant to
be judged to allow you to access Paradise.

*May the Most High soften your heart even more
and grant you an ocean of love.*
آمين

A few gentle words from your sisters...

The following words come from some of your sisters.

In the darkness, His light shines
brightest.
We realize that life is but a trial that
will lead us back to Him.
The fierce struggle against our souls
may often make us falter, but victories
will also be frequent.

Thus, in times of disorder, He is the One encouraging
you not to give up. Your Lord has neither scorned nor
abandoned you.
Draw closer to Him in these dark moments, and your
soul will endure even more.
Patience, O troubled soul, the outcome is near.

May the Most Merciful make His light your aid.
آمين

When everything darkens and you no longer feel
safe: open your eyes, listen to the words of your
Lord.
Do not remain in darkness when you can no
longer see the good in this world.
Be like a candle in the night, seek the light, and
you will see that Allah has always shown you the
clear path.
He is your guide, and from Him, never despair.

Endure patiently, my sister.
Not everything is sadness.
Allah is never inattentive to your
distress.

Assia Slimani

On the road to Allah, the journey will
certainly be very challenging.
Do not forget His words that teach us that
after every difficulty comes ease.
You will need to learn not to care about the
people who will prevent you from getting
closer to Him.

As a result, you may feel very lonely at times,
but isn't *solitude better than harmful company?*

Sometimes you may stop along the way, but the
most important thing is that you keep going.
Hold on tight, my dear, and have faith in Him.

*May the Most High increase your faith on
this journey.*
آمين

Life is a minefield.
Sometimes you will find yourself walking along unlit paths, and you will have no choice but to use them.
You will think they never end, but they do.
Righteousness leads to Allah.
What He sees is not the number of times you get lost, but how much you hope in prayer that He will come to your rescue even if your heart is at war.
Do not spend a day without thinking of Him by your side. Allah is the only One who can guide you.
In His Paradise, your soul will find rest. And indeed, your existence is but a long journey, yet its destiny is truth.

May the words of Allah be your guiding light here and in the hereafter.

Assia Slimani

All the injustices you have endured, Allah is
aware of them..
He knows everything you do not, especially
the deepest intentions of people's hearts.

The day when every soul returns to Him, true
justice will prevail.

Be patient for a little while longer, do not harm
yourself, He will establish your rights with
your oppressors.
Do not cry, He sees you. Show Him the
strength of your faith.

May the Most High keep you away from injustice.
آمين

*Can you hear the birds singing and the
soothing sound of their words?
Do not they go straight to your heart to take
away all your fears?*

It is possible that anger challenges you on
this earth, that injustices overwhelm you,
and in the world, you would like to scream to
be left in peace.
But it is in these moments that you must
confide in the Confidant and read His words
to finally be understood.
Allah is the best companion on the road,
never doubt Him.
He is always near you and listening.

*Read in the name of your Lord so that your heart is
calmed of your fears, and it blossoms like a flower.*

Assia Slimani

Theres a famous quote from The Little Prince: "One sees clearly only with the heart. Anything essential is invisible to the eyes."

Be one of those gentle souls who express themselves only with kindness and benevolence.
May your words reflect the goodness of your heart and the purity of your soul.
Do not let the darkness of others darken your heart, much less weaken your faith.

The good you sow will return to you.
Your Lord sees you.
So, do not worry.

May the Most High allow you to do nothing but good.
آمين

There are people who can see with their soul
and not just with their eyes.
Their words come from the heart, not just
the tongue.
Cultivate the gentleness in your words and
sow the fragrance of goodness.

*May the Almighty be pleased with you, with who
you are.*
آمين

Assia Slimani

No matter what anyone assures you, the course
of your life depends solely on what Allah has
decreed. You will constantly be urged to take
paths that are not yours, to utter words that do
not reflect you, and to make decisions that
should not be made.

Do not be afraid to let go of what does not
suit you.
Be the person you want to be, the person you
aspire to be.
You have the power and the ability!
You just need to understand and accept it.

Do not spoil the beauty that slumbers within you.
Let it blossom so you can shine.

May the Lord embellish your heart.
آمين

We tend to put aside the one that accompanies
us on our journey through life.
Give your soul a dose of tenderness.
Give it what you would like others to give you,
without expecting anything from anyone.
It is up to you to take action to change your
situation and find peace.

*May Allah open the doors of repentance for your
soul so that you can leave with the good news of His
Paradise and may He accept you.*
آمين

Assia Slimani

He is the One who will silence the noise in
your heart.
He is the only One who can totally soothe
your soul of all the evils of this life.
He will never stop loving you as long as you
love Him in return.
He is the One who will protect you from those who
wish your misfortune; as long as you put your
trust in Him, you have nothing to fear.

Never cease to be grateful to Him for all the
blessings He bestows upon you and for the
security He offers you.

*May the Most High make love for Him reign in
your heart.*
آمين

He loved you before you were born,
He still loves you today and will love you
tomorrow with His immense grace.
He is the one who revives your heart like a
spark of light in a dark night, the hope when
chaos ensues, and the love when His
creatures try to break you.
I pray that your heart and soul be filled with
His love.

*May Allah grant you all His love and may no one
extinguish the light that is yours.*
آمين

Your sister Farrah, with all her love.

And even when your soul seems to be broken,
do not cease to hope, for your Lord only tests
you for your own good.

He never burdens you beyond your capacity.
The sorrows you have overcome will only
revive the beauty of your soul.

They are but temporary pains for you.
You are full of kindness, do not let any hurt
turn you away from it.

Invoke Him, He will soothe you.

*May the Lord of the Worlds ease your deepest
wounds and elevate your soul to the highest degree of
His Paradise.*
آمين

I pray that every part of your soul will be rebuilt in the best possible way, that every crack in your soul will find its charm and strength when you see a flaw in it.
 I pray for you, for I have been taught to love Allah above all else.

May Allah elevate your soul.
آمين

Farrah

When you speak, make sure to speak only good.
Otherwise, silence is the best advisor.
Words slip from us so easily and yet their consequences can be disastrous.
Take care of that piece of flesh, your tongue; it could save many already pained hearts.

Your Lord has certainly taught you kindness and brotherhood.
Everyone has a role to play.
Now it is your turn to comfort your sisters with words full of love and kindness.

One day, you will be the one who needs it,
Would you like a sister to do it for you?

May the Most High soften your tongue.
آمين

Do not let words or actions hurt you. Do not
let trials kill you, for surely, Allah tests those
He loves.
Be patient and learn to endure, for the
reward is beyond your expectations.
And even if you feel alone, you are never
truly alone.
The Mighty, the Majestic, the Glorious is by
your side, and believe me, you need nothing
more than Him.

*May the Lord soothe your heart of countless
pains.*
آمين

Anonymous

Do you know the true value of patience?

If humans truly knew its worth, they would
never tire of being patient.
They would implore their Lord to extend their
trials so that their patience could be further
tested.
Exercising patience allows the soul to grow.
Moreover, the longer the patience, the greater
the reward. This is just one of the many
blessings bestowed upon you by your Lord.
Learn to appreciate it, as it can only benefit you.

May the Most High grant you great patience.
آمين

Patience, such a sweet word that allows you
to be serene at every moment of your life.

It is a real strength, accessible to everyone,
which is cultivated throughout one's life.
Patience requires courage, and I am
convinced that deep down inside you, you
possess this courage in abundance.

To entrust everything to Allah, to take action, to
seek His help, and to patiently endure. Every
aspect of our lives has been decreed by Him, and
everything will unfold according to His will.

Take care of your soul, nurture it towards
righteousness, teach it to be patient and
resilient to make it stronger and more
steadfast by the permission of the Almighty.

*May Allah grant you the patience and courage
to overcome your trials.*
Ameen

A., your sister who loves you for the sake of Allah.

There is an emptiness in your heart that can
only be filled with love for your Creator.
Until you give Him His due, this feeling
will never go away.

The further away you are from Him, the more
likely it is that your heart will harden.
He is the One who saves you from distress
and grants you tranquility.

Believers do not despair of His mercy
and hope for a good end.
Be among those who are devoted and rely on
Him alone.
The long river that is your life will gradually
calm down.

May Allah bring you as close to Him as possible.
آمين

Read His words when you feel that emptiness.
Listen to His words when you feel your heart
being torn apart by memories.
He will save you from your sorrows and tears.

It will get better, do not worry.
Do not give up, Allah is with you.
He is with those who endure and those
who firmly believe in His existence.

Do not be one of those who no longer believe,
but among those who believe even the more.

*May Allah unite us in the highest level of
Paradise.*
آمين

Anonymous

Dear gentle soul in trial,
Use this sadness to make others happy.
You are in the best position to know what
you would like to hear; pass it on. You will
likely do much good, perhaps even be a
source of comfort through your words.
Thus, your Lord will reward you for this
beautiful treasure you offer comforting
your sister in Allah.

*Isn't it a wonderful gift to relieve the pain
of a believer?*

Patience... Your Creator will turn your sadness
into great joy and will certainly grant you His
Paradise as long as you constantly rely on Him.

*May the Most Merciful make your sadness an
expiation of sins and allow you to be a source of
comfort for your sisters.*
آمين

My sister in faith,

I know how much your heart pounds and weeps.
I know how lonely you feel, perhaps even
abandoned by your Creator.
But remember one thing: He loves you so much, and
I know you do too.
Do not stop shining.
Show your gratitude to your Lord and He will give
you what you wish for.

He has chosen you and guided you to the
right path. You are among those He loves.

Do not give Him the opportunity to stray you
and please, don't postpone things until
tomorrow.
Pray, pray, pray to your Lord.
You can be called back at any moment.

*May He who answers the call of the needy and the
desirous answer your prayers.*
آمين

Anonymous

To whoever reads this, know that deliverance is near. With the help of Allah, you are capable of overcoming any trial, any pain, any sorrow. By drawing closer to your Lord, your problems will be lighter to bear, and you will live through your trials with the conviction that Allah is with the patient and that He loves you.

This worldly life is made of tests to prepare our abode in the hereafter. It is up to you, my sister, to be strong and to have the love of Allah in your heart.

Whatever you do, do it for Allah above all, for your faith. Do good around you and this good will be rewarded by His permission.
Try to be optimistic and do not let certain wasawis take over your mind, you are stronger than that.
Do not forget that happiness resides with Allah.

May Allah fill your heart with joy and peace.
آمين

A. Your sister who loves you for the sake of Allah.

In this worldly life, you will always need to
show courage and kindness.
Be courageous in the face of every trial. Never
lose hope or patience.

And you know that He is there, close to you,
and He will never abandon you.
Keep trust in Him and always have a good
opinion of Him.

Know that behind every situation lies a good.
Accept destiny whether it is good or bad and
say Al hamduliLlah for everything.

Remain kind no matter what!
Being malicious darkens hearts and only harms
yourself.
It attracts Shaytan towards you, and your heart
cannot bear all this.
While being kind soothes your heart and the
hearts of others

Respond to evil with goodness.
Do not worry, your kindness will be seen by Allah, and you will be rewarded for it.
And that is all that matters; only His perspective counts and will count in the Hereafter.
Do it for Him.

Have courage in the face of all this, be strong and hang in there.
I assure you, it is worth it, you cannot imagine all that awaits you, In shaa Allah.

May Allah grant you the greatest reward for your patience, courage and strength. Take care of your heart, be courageous and kind.
آمين

May sweetness permeate your soul

We are neither scholars nor students of religious science. Therefore, we preferred to avoid delving into detail in our words, as we do not have the necessary religious knowledge.
However, we wanted to convey certain words that could soothe your hearts.

I sincerely hope that many souls will find comfort in this book. That's all I wish for.
I love you for the sake of Allah, my sisters, and even if we Do not know each other, take care of yourselves.

P-S: For those of you who only know me through this book, feel free to take a look at my first book, *"Soothe your heart and bloom your soul : Kindness and tenderness "*, which tells the story of my depression and much more...

Kind regards,

Lilya B.F | @douceurandsabr_

Lilya B.F
Contactprolbf@gmail.com

Correction service | Rewriting, proofreading and correction
servicedecorrection1@gmail.com

Layout and proofreading
oumma-correction@outlook.fr

May sweetness permeate your soul

May sweetness permeate your soul